# GRANNY
## GET YOUR
# GLUE GUN

### HOW TO HAVE FUN
### WITH YOUR GRANDCHILDREN

**MAUREEN GOULET & DIANA BUDDEN**

To our much cherished offspring –
Carrie and Matthew, Jessie, Clare and Grant –
who will, no doubt, provide us with some amazing
grandchildren – sooner or later.

Madi Publishing
A Division of Ambrosia Adventures In Cooking Ltd &
NPA Infrastructure Financial Services Ltd
West Vancouver, BC, Canada
www.grannygetyourgluegun.com

ISBN 978-0-9948097-0-4

Cataloguing in Publication data available from
Library and Archives Canada

Cover illustration: Simon Meyers, www.prettyfunky.com
Interior design: Vivalogue Publishing (Canada) Ltd
Photography: Hamid Attie, Mike Wakefield, Diana Budden & Maureen Goulet

DISCLAIMER:
While the authors have highlighted any significant health and safety issues
involved with the activities and crafts described in this book, users are
responsible for ensuring the safety of those participating. The authors
disclaim any liability whatsoever with respect to any loss, injury or damage
arising out of the use of the information contained in this book or omission
from any information in this book.

Printed in Canada

# CONTENTS

Introduction _____ 5

Craft Box _____ 7

Dress-up Box _____ 8

Creative Crafts _____ 10

   Gift Bags _____ 11

   Grandma's Smelly Dough _____ 12

   Flubber _____ 14

   Elephant Toothpaste _____ 15

   Growth Chart _____ 17

   Personalized Place Mat _____ 18

   Piñata _____ 21

   Toilet Roll Feeder _____ 23

   Paper Chain Necklace _____ 25

   Popsicle Stick Jigsaw Puzzles _____ 26

   Wine Cork Boat _____ 27

   Sweet Dreams Pillowcase _____ 28

   Simple Stained Glass Ornaments _____ 29

In the Kitchen _____ 30

   Dog Treats _____ 31

   5-Minute Chocolate Cake in a Mug _____ 32

   Homemade Ice Cream _____ 33

   Ice Cream Cone Cupcakes _____ 35

   Simple Fondant _____ 36

   Chilled Mint Tea _____ 37

   Marshmallows _____ 38

Great Games _____ 40

   Fishing Game _____ 41

   Indoor Fort _____ 42

   Dancing Ping Pong Balls _____ 43

   Fortune Teller _____ 44

   Talking Cans _____ 46

QUICK 'N' EASY ........................................................................ 48

    Card Houses ........................................................ 49

    Marshmallow Engineers .................................... 49

    Pretend Camera ................................................. 49

    Hide a Little Toy ............................................... 50

    Invisible Painting ............................................... 50

    Coins in the Garden .......................................... 51

    Dancing Diving Raisins ...................................... 51

    Make Your Own Butter ..................................... 52

    Animals in the House ......................................... 52

    Sticky Note Treasure Hunt .............................. 53

    Window Picasso ................................................. 55

LET'S CHILL! ......................................................................... 56

    Lip-Smacking Lip Gloss ..................................... 57

    Egg White Mini-Facial ...................................... 58

    Super Soak Detox Footbath ............................ 59

    Bubble Jelly Bath Gel ...................................... 61

ABOUT THE AUTHORS ........................................................ 62

# INTRODUCTION

*Are you asking yourself, "How in the world am I going to entertain my visiting grandchildren?" GRANNY GET YOUR GLUE GUN is here to help!*

Today's grandparents are busy, vibrant people whose lives are filled with friends and activities. At the same time, many grandmas and grandpas are ready and only too willing to help out their children by spending time with the grandchildren.

GRANNY GET YOUR GLUE GUN provides you with a variety of entertaining activities to make the precious time you spend with your grandchildren both fun and creative. To help you preserve some of those lovely memories of times shared, we have provided places to attach photos of the creations you make together and to record those memorable words "from the mouths of babes." We'd like you to use and enjoy GRANNY GET YOUR GLUE GUN as a keepsake book as well as a practical activity guide.

We've given you a guide to the basics you'll need to enjoy creative crafts, fun in the kitchen, great games and quick 'n' easy activities, plus pleasant ways to relax with the grandkids. For each activity, we provide appropriate ages, approximate preparation time, lists of supplies and ingredients, and clear, step-by-step instructions to minimize fuss and maximize fun.

Our aim is for all you amazing grandparents to really enjoy getting down-and-dirty with those little bundles of joy, your very own grandchildren.

*Grab that glue gun, roll up those sleeves and let the fun begin!*

## USING THIS BOOK

AGE: only suggestions. You will know the capabilities of your own grandchildren.

TIME: these are approximate preparation times. You may find some take longer depending on how many questions your grandchildren come up with!

SUPPLIES: a lot of the supplies are readily available at your local dollar stores, craft and fabric stores.

WARNINGS: are there to alert you to possible hazards. The activities in this book are designed to be child-friendly but some of them will involve closer supervision than others.

IDEAS: suggestions to take your craft or activity to new and different levels.

Make decorating the new craft box with your grandchild your first project!

# CRAFT BOX

*Crafts are a great way to keep little hands busy and can help to develop creativity in your grandchildren. Be prepared!*

Use a sturdy box – wood, cardboard or plastic – to store at least the basic supplies so they're ready at hand. Ideally, the box should be large enough to hold a variety of papers so they can lie flat, with lots of room for other items. You can pick up additional supplies for some of the activities the day before or make it a special shopping outing with your grandchild.

## USEFUL EXTRAS

wide popsicle sticks (plain & coloured) • toothpicks • toilet & paper towel rolls • egg cartons • yoghurt containers • wrapping paper scraps • old magazines • tin foil & wax paper • brown paper sandwich bags • straws • paper plates • googly eyes • wool & thread • paper clips & safety pins • string & ribbons • beads & sequins • clear contact paper sheets • iron-on fusible bonding web • etc, etc

*You are sure to be the queen or king of crafts so don't forget to make yourself a crown!*

*Grandparents are there to help the child get into mischief they haven't thought of yet.* GENE PERRET

## BASICS

paper: inexpensive drawing/computer paper for crayon & pencil use

heavier quality paper for painting & markers

coloured construction paper & heavy card stock

paints: washable, tempera & acrylic (in pots or tin boxes)

brushes: variety of sizes & qualities (cheap ones for gluing)

glue: sticks, PVA glue (white glue)

tape: clear sticky tape, masking tape

crayons, coloured pencils, lead pencils & felt-tip markers

scissors: safety (kid-friendly) & better ones for grandma

glue gun

hole punch

sparkles

## BASICS

suit jackets, pants

dresses, skirts, blouses

old uniforms

old Halloween costumes

shoes, boots, low heels

hats, wigs, tiaras

headbands, veils

boas, wands, wings

necklaces, Mardi Gras beads, leis

small box for jewellery

clip-on earrings

**!**

Make sure the box lid is light enough not to injure hands or heads if it falls down! .

# DRESS-UP BOX

*Our children spent many wonderful hours playing with clothes from the Dress-Up Box. In fact, they still come home, pre-Halloween, to raid its contents!*

Pick a large, lightweight box with a hinged lid that is sturdy enough to stand the test of time.

A great place to start your collection is from your own closets. Thrift shops, discount stores and garage sales all provide a wealth of inexpensive choices to add to your box. Your box should contain a balance of boys' and girls' items.

Children will play for hours dressing up, especially if your box is filled with imaginative supplies. They will want to be rummaging in there every time they come over!

## USEFUL EXTRAS

mirror • apron • hairbrush/comb • rubber gloves • old cell phone • keys • play money • doctor or nurse kit • magnifying glass • toy microphone • etc, etc

*You can play dress up too! Get out the good silver and have a tea party with your well-dressed little friends!*

*A grandmother pretends she doesn't know who you are at Halloween.* ERMA BOMBECK

TIPS

Cut down length of long dresses with pinking shears to avoid tripping.

Replace buttons with Velcro for easy on and off.

# GIFT BAGS

*Everyone loves a little surprise inside a pretty bag*

AGE • 6+    TIME • 45 MIN

1. Fold over top of lunch bag approx 2 inches (5 cm).
2. Punch two holes, 1 inch (2.5 cm) apart, through all layers of paper.
3. Iron fusible bonding onto back side of fabric.
4. Cut out shapes around fabric designs.
5. Remove backing from fusible bonding and iron cut-out shape directly onto bag.
6. If using old greeting cards, cut out design and glue or hot glue onto bag.
7. Place small gift or treats inside, then thread ribbon or raffia through holes from back of bag so you have two equal lengths.
8. Tie ribbon/raffia into a bow.

*Create a collection of these to use as goodie bags at the next birthday party!*

*I don't intentionally spoil my grandkids. It's just that correcting them often takes more energy than I have left.* GENE PERRET

# GRANDMA'S SMELLY DOUGH

*Don't worry kids, the real dough is in the bank!*

AGE • 2+   TIME • 20 MIN

1. Mix flour, salt, drink mix and cream of tartar in a bowl.
2. Boil water in microwave or saucepan.
3. In separate bowl, combine boiled water and oil.
4. Add dry ingredients and mix with spoon until cool enough to knead.
5. Knead until colour is blended.
6. Store in airtight bag or container in refrigerator.

*Playing with this dough is good for little growing hands and old arthritic ones.*

*It's amazing how young grandparents seem once you become one.* ANON

To make Christmas ornaments, omit drink mix and use seasonal-shaped cookie cutters. Insert a hook in top. Slow bake in oven (300-325°F/150-160°C) until firm. Decorate with paint or markers.

FLUBBER, page 14

# FLUBBER

*Call yourself "The Absent-Minded Professor"! This smooth, elastic-like substance goes from solid to liquid and back again with slight temperature changes*

AGE • 3+    TIME • 10 MIN

1. In one bowl, combine cold water, glue, food colouring and glitter (if using). Set aside.
2. In other bowl, combine hot water and borax. Stir until borax is completely dissolved.
3. Slowly add glue mixture to borax mixture.
4. Combine well until mixture forms a ball and pulls away from sides of bowl. Drain off any excess liquid.
5. Knead until smooth and elastic.
6. Shape into a ball or drape over mouth of a jar and see what happens.

*Now you are ready for hours of playing with this goop!*

*An hour with the grandchildren can make you feel young again. Anything more and you will age more quickly.* GENE PERRET

Photo page 13

## SUPPLIES

2 medium bowls

3/4 c cold water (180 ml)

1 c PVA (white) glue (250ml)

1/2 c hot water (125 ml)

1 tsp borax (5 ml)

food colouring & glitter (optional)

## TIPS

Borax is a laundry-booster found in most grocery stores.

Store in a sealable bag or jar to keep it from drying out

Vinegar dissolves Flubber from carpets, hair, clothes, pets, etc.

**!**

Keep out of children's mouths!

# ELEPHANT TOOTHPASTE

*You are about to make a fantastic foaming fountain!*

AGE • 6+    TIME • 5 MIN

1. Mix yeast into warm water. Set aside for 5 minutes.
2. Place bottle on tray or in sink. Using a funnel, fill with hydrogen peroxide.
3. Add dish soap to bottle and swirl gently to combine.
4. Add 6-10 drops of food colouring gel and glitter (if using). For a rainbow effect, carefully drip different colours of food colouring down inside of bottle.
5. Stand bottle in a larger dish or in sink.
6. Using funnel, add yeast mixture to bottle.
7. Quickly remove funnel and watch results!

*Holy foaming toothpaste, Batman!*

*Elephants and grandchildren never forget.*
ANDY ROONEY

Ambitious types could create a papier mâché volcano around the bottle. Finish the volcano with shellac or varnish if you want to re-use it. For more dramatic results, use 6% hydrogen peroxide. Follow cautions on bottle.

### SUPPLIES

1 pkg active dry yeast (8 g)

2 tbsp warm water (30 ml)

1/2 c hydrogen peroxide 3% solution 10 volume (125 ml)

funnel

narrow- necked bottle (approx 16 oz/500 ml)

food colouring gel & glitter (optional)

1/4 cup liquid dish soap (60 ml)

**!**

Adult supervision required

Add names and heights of other friends and family members. And don't forget your pets!

# Growth Chart

*Keep track of those sprouting children who seem to grow up all too quickly.*

AGE • ALL   TIME • 40 MIN

1. Tape cards together, on the back side, to make one long strip.
2. With chart lying flat, using ruler or yardstick, start from bottom and mark off inches and feet or centimetres. Repeat until you reach top of chart. Go over pencil lines with markers in one or more colours, labelling bolder lines at the foot levels.
3. Decorate your chart with favourite stickers or pictures, leaving space for names and dates.
4. To hang growth chart temporarily, punch two holes at top and make an adjustable length tie so it can hang on a hook from a door.

*Look out, Grandma – those kids grow like weeds!*

*A grandfather is someone with silver in his hair and gold in his heart.* ANON

## SUPPLIES

5 letter-sized sheets of coloured heavy card stock

ruler or yardstick

masking or clear tape

pencil

felt-tip markers

stickers or cut-out pictures

hole punch

string or ribbon

## TIPS

You can also clip chart to a wire hanger with clothes pegs.

Reinforce edges by folding extra wide clear tape lengthwise along edge.

# PERSONALIZED PLACE MAT

*A personal place mat will always make your grandchild feel at home!*

AGE • 3+ TIME • 30-60 MIN

1. Cut cardboard into a 13 inch x 18 inch piece (33 cm x 46 cm) or use an existing place mat as a template.
2. Cut out pictures from magazines and photos for decoration.
3. Arrange pictures on cardboard, then glue in position.
4. Write name and date on cardboard.
5. Once glue is dry, place cardboard over 2 sheets of clear contact paper. Using cardboard as a template, cut 2 sheets 1 inch larger than cardboard all round.

## SUPPLIES

1 sheet heavy card stock

magazines

photos

felt-tip markers

crayons

scissors

glue stick

2 sheets clear contact paper or vinyl sleeve

## TIP

Outline child's hands and/or feet with pencil. Then colour pencil marks with felt-tip markers/ crayons

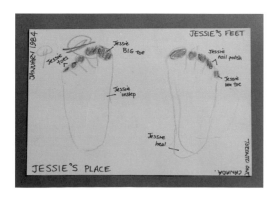

Kate, age 3

July 25, 2015

6. Peel protective layer off one sheet and lay on table, sticky side up. Place decorated cardboard, face down, onto sticky sheet. Press firmly.

7. Peel protective layer off second sheet and press on undecorated side of cardboard. Press hard around edges to seal and flatten. Trim if necessary.

Additional photo page 30

*Hey, Grandma! Where do I sit?*

*Grandma always makes you feel she has been waiting to see you all day and now the day is complete.* MARY DEMAREE

# PIÑATA

*Every year we made a piñata filled with candy for my children's birthday parties. They are a great way to end the event!* MG

AGES • 3+        TIME • 30-60 MIN (+ DRYING TIME)

1. Making your piñata can get a little messy, so be sure you give yourself plenty of space. Cover your work area with layers of newspaper or a disposable plastic tablecloth.
2. Inflate and tie off balloon.
3. Tear newspaper into strips, 1-2 inches x 6-8 inches (approx 3-6 x 9-18 cm). You need enough strips to cover balloon with several layers.
4. Mix together flour, water and salt in bowl to make papier mâché paste. Stir mixture until it starts to thicken into a relatively smooth batter.
5. Dip paper strips into paste, removing excess paste by running strips through your pinched fingers or dragging them along edge of bowl. (Remove as much excess paste as possible.)

## SUPPLIES

1 bowl

1 c flour (250 ml)

1 c cold water (250 ml)

1 tbsp salt (15 ml)

newspaper

1 medium-sized balloon

string

paint

candy (lots!)

streamers, paper flowers (optional)

## TIPS

To prevent inflated balloon from rolling around, balance it in a bowl while applying strips.

Use a paintbrush to coat strips with paste.

6. Apply strips to balloon, crisscrossing them until entire balloon is covered. Leave knot of balloon uncovered.
7. Repeat previous step to make 3 to 4 layers. Tie string to knot of balloon and hang piñata to dry.
8. When completely dry (approx 2 hours), paint or decorate piñata.
9. If balloon has not yet popped, pop it and remove.
10. Make hole big enough to stuff candy into piñata and fill with candy.
11. Punch two small holes close to main hole.
12. Tie string or ribbon through holes to create a loop long enough to suspend piñata from ceiling or from a long stick.
13. Decorate piñata with streamers, paper flowers or anything else.
14. Cover hole with paper or masking tape to keep goodies inside!

*You are now ready to let those kids whack away (with some supervision) at your beautiful piñata!*

*My grandmother was a very tough woman. She buried three husbands and two of them were just napping.* RITA RUDNER

! Contents will be scattered on the ground, so avoid anything breakable or very small

# TOILET ROLL FEEDER

*Your feathered friends and four-footed creatures will love you for this!*

AGE • 2+          TIME • 15 MIN

### SUPPLIES

toilet roll

1/2 c peanut butter (125 ml)

plate

1/2 c birdseed (125 ml)

1. Cover toilet roll evenly with peanut butter using a small knife or spatula.
2. Pour birdseed onto plate (paper is good for easy clean-up).
3. Roll coated toilet roll in birdseed until well covered, pressing seed into peanut butter.
4. Stick roll onto a bare branch outside and watch for hungry birds and squirrels!

*Warning: elephants are attracted to peanut butter, so hang this feeder high in the trees!*

### TIP

If no branches are available, run a string through tube and hang it.

*Do you know why grandchildren are always so full of energy? They suck it out of their grandparents.* GENE PERRET

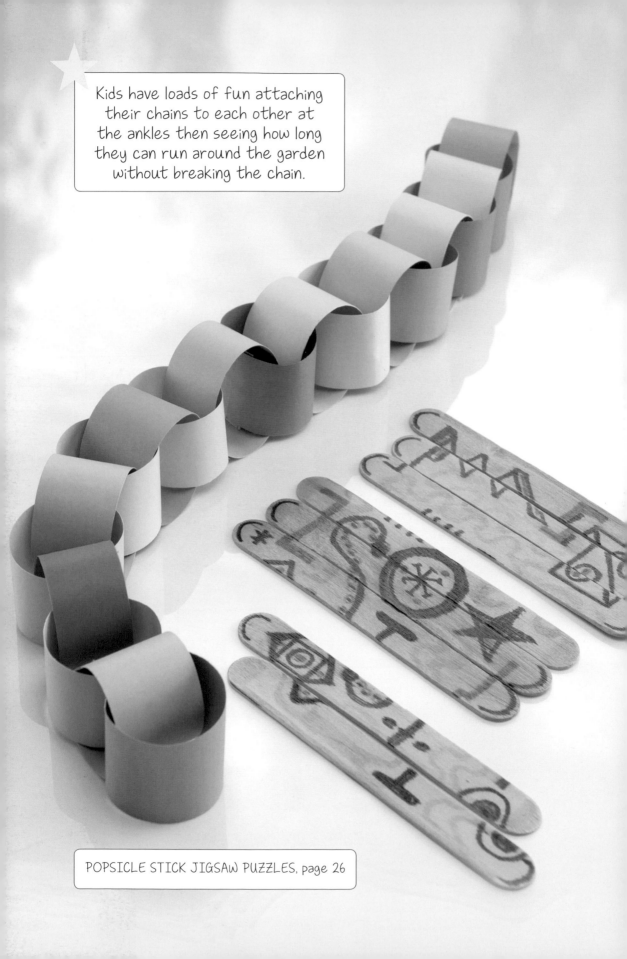

Kids have loads of fun attaching their chains to each other at the ankles then seeing how long they can run around the garden without breaking the chain.

POPSICLE STICK JIGSAW PUZZLES, page 26

# PAPER CHAIN NECKLACE

*Here's something easy for both grand-parent and grandchild! If you are lovin' it, carry on and create an endless chain.*

AGE • 3+          TIME • 30 MIN

SUPPLIES

coloured construction paper

pencil

ruler

scissors

PVA (white) glue, stapler or tape

1. With pencil and ruler, mark off strips on different coloured papers, approx 1/2 x 3 inches (1.25 x 8 cm).
2. Cut about 30 strips.
3. Make first loop by overlapping ends and securing them with glue, tape or staple.
4. Place second strip through first loop and join ends.
5. Continue adding one strip/loop at a time until your chain has grown to desired length.

*The original chain gang!*

*The best place to be when you're sad is Grandma's lap.* ANON

This can also make a great Christmas tree decoration or Christmas countdown chain. Number the loops 1 to 24. Starting Dec 1, remove a link each day until it's time for Santa to arrive!

# POPSICLE STICK JIGSAW PUZZLES

*Collecting the sticks is half the fun!*

AGE • 3+          TIME • 30-60 MIN

## SUPPLIES

1 pkg flat popsicle sticks or tongue depressors

masking tape

felt-tip markers

crayons

## TIP

Number each stick on back side to help with reassembly later, if necessary.

Write a "secret" message across taped-together sticks. Remove tape and mail loose sticks to a friend who must solve puzzle to read message.

Photo page 24

1. Give each child 8 sticks.
2. Arrange sticks, laying them flat, side-by-side.
3. Secure sticks with two strips of masking tape to prevent them from moving.
4. Flip over and create a design on front of sticks. Design should cross over sticks in various directions.
5. When happy with the puzzle design, remove tape from back.
6. Jumble up sticks and get kids to put puzzles together again.

*Puzzles challenge our problem-solving skills and keep aging minds engaged and active!*

*I wish I had the energy that my grandchildren have – if only for self-defence.* GENE PERRET

# WINE CORK BOAT

*This is will explain why you have so many empty wine bottles.*

AGE • 3+          TIME • 30 MIN

1. Lie corks side by side. Wrap corks together using rubber bands.
2. Pierce paper square twice and insert toothpick for mast and sail.
3. Push toothpick with sail into middle cork of boat.

*Watch out for sharks and pirates, Matey!*

### SUPPLIES

3 wine corks

2 rubber bands

card stock

clear contact paper (optional)

toothpick

### TIPS

Laminate paper square with contact paper to make it waterproof.

If you are planning to use your boat in a creek or lake, attach a length of string to keep boat from floating away.

*My grandmother is over eighty and still doesn't need glasses. Drinks straight out of the bottle.* HENNY YOUNGMAN

# SWEET DREAMS PILLOWCASE

## SUPPLIES

1 cotton pillowcase

crayons (fabric crayons work best)

1 sheet cardboard

paper towels

iron

## TIPS

Wash pillowcase cold water and tumble dry on low before first use.

If you are not an aspiring artist, follow steps 4 and 5 of Gift Bags (page 11) and iron a design onto pillowcase!

Photo page 42

*Visions of grandma and grandpa will dance in their heads – sweet dreams!*

AGE • 3+          TIME • 30-60 MIN

1. Draw a large heart in centre of pillowcase with crayon. Be sure to go over it a few times to make colour strong.
2. Place cardboard inside pillowcase.
3. Have children draw pictures of their happy thoughts in middle of heart.
4. Write child's name in crayon on pillowcase.
5. Cover drawings/heart with paper towel.
6. With iron on medium setting, iron paper towel for at least one minute.
7. Lift paper towel to see if wax has melted into fabric. If necessary, repeat previous step with a fresh piece of towel to get crayon absorbed into fabric.

*Use your grandchild's Sweet Dreams Pillowcase for sleepovers at your home.*

*Grandchildren don't make a man feel old; it's the knowledge that he is married to a grandmother.* G. NORMAN COLLIE

# SIMPLE STAINED GLASS ORNAMENTS

*These little suncatchers will brighten up your day when your little rays of sunshine have gone home!*

SUPPLIES

coloured tissue paper

marker

2 sheets clear contact paper

clear tape

scissors

AGE • 3+        TIME • 15 MIN

1. Cut or tear bright coloured tissue paper into shapes or bits.
2. On non-sticky side of contact paper sheet, draw a variety of large shapes.
3. Peel off protective layer from sheet and tape it, sticky side up, to table.
4. Place tissue bits and shapes inside the drawn shapes, leaving a small margin.
5. Peel off protective layer from second piece of contact paper and cover design, pressing down firmly.
6. Cut out ornaments in shapes of diamonds, circles, etc.
7. Hang ornaments in window.

Cut out shapes for each holiday – hearts, Easter eggs, shamrocks – to help make your home more festive

*Let the sun shine in!*

*I have a role now that I think becomes me. I am a grandparent.* SARA PERETSKY

Pet Treats

Used to Show Love

Intended as an occasional treat
or indulgence and not the sole
source of the animal's nutrition

PERSONALIZED PLACE MAT, page 18

# DOG TREATS

*Selling these cookies at a local craft fair earned my son enough money to buy himself a brand new, shiny bike.* MG

AGE • 3+          TIME • 45 MIN          YIELD • 2 DOZEN

1. Preheat oven to 350°F/180°C.
2. Combine flour and cornmeal in a bowl or food processor.
3. Add oil, broth, 1 egg, milk powder and water. Mix until it forms a ball. If still sticky, add more flour.
4. Roll out dough on floured surface to 1/4-inch thickness.
5. Cut into assorted fun shapes.
6. Place cut cookies on parchment paper-lined cookie sheet.
7. Whisk other egg, mix with 1 tbsp (15 ml) water and brush tops of cookies.
8. Bake 15-20 min or until golden brown. Cool completely.

*You will have him eating out of your hand!*

*If I had known how wonderful it would be to have grandchildren, I'd have had them first.* LOIS WYSE

### SUPPLIES

1 c whole wheat flour (250 ml)

1/3 c cornmeal (80 ml)

bowl or food processor

1 tbsp canola oil (15 ml)

1/4 c beef broth (60 ml)

2 eggs

1/4 c skim milk powder (60 ml)

1/4 c water (60 ml)

rolling pin

cookie cutters

cookie sheet

parchment paper

Cut out gingerbread men and use beef jerky for eyes. Place in canine's Christmas stocking.

# 5-MINUTE CHOCOLATE CAKE IN A MUG

*Snack time for everyone! Kids will love making their own mini-cake and then gobbling it up!*

AGE • 3+        TIME • 5 MIN

1. Combine dry ingredients in mug and mix well.
2. Add egg, milk and oil. Mix well.
3. Add chocolate chips (optional) and vanilla. Mix well.
4. Fill mug no more than 2/3 full with batter (do not overfill).
5. Cook in microwave for 3 min on high.
6. Cake may rise over lip of the mug. CAREFULLY remove from microwave as cup will be VERY hot! Allow to cool.
7. Enjoy straight out of mug or tip it out onto a plate to share.

*YUMMMM...*

*My grandmother started walking five miles a day when she was 60. She's 97 now and we don't know where the hell she is.*
ELLEN DEGENERES

## SUPPLIES

4 tbsp flour (60 ml)

3 tbsp sugar (45 ml)

2 tbsp cocoa (30 ml)

1 egg

3 tbsp milk (45 ml)

1 tbsp oil (15 ml)

3 tbsp chocolate chips (45 ml), optional

1 splash vanilla

coffee mug (microwave safe)

## TIP

For easier cleanup in case of overflow, place mug on saucer or plate.

Add Homemade Ice Cream (page 33) for extra decadence!

# HOMEMADE ICE CREAM

*This could be very dangerous for your waistline!*

AGE • 3+     TIME • 10-20 MIN     YIELD • 1 CUP

1. Combine milk, sugar and vanilla in medium sealable freezer bag. Seal, leaving a little air, and shake.
2. Put ice and salt into large freezer bag. Shake to combine.
3. Place sealed smaller bag with milk mixture into larger bag. Seal tight.
4. Slosh bags back and forth across your countertop until contents thicken into ice cream. (Be careful not to press too hard on bags or seals will break.)
5. Remove small bag from larger one and store ice cream in freezer,

*Grab a spoon and just eat it right out of the bag!*

*When grandparents enter the door, discipline flies out the window.* OGDEN NASH

## SUPPLIES

1 c whole milk or whipping cream (250 ml)

2 tbsp sugar (30 ml)

1/4 tsp vanilla (1 ml), or other flavouring

1 large sealable freezer bag (3.78 L)

1 medium sealable freezer bag (0.94 L)

1/4 c coarse salt (pickling or rock) (60 ml)

2 c ice (500 ml)

## TIP

Use non-dairy milk if lactose intolerant.

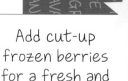

Add cut-up frozen berries for a fresh and fruity ice cream.

# ICE CREAM CONE CUPCAKES

*These cones will not melt, even on the hottest day. We have both made these for children's birthdays, no plates needed. Kids can run around the garden and drop them anywhere!*

AGE • 4+        TIME • 35 MIN

1. Preheat oven to 350°F/180°C.
2. Prepare cake mix (reducing suggested oil amount by 1/2), or make your own favourite basic cake recipe.
3. Spoon batter into each cone to 2/3 full.
4. Stand cones in muffin tin with crumpled foil around cones to hold them steady.
5. Bake about 20 min or until toothpick inserted into centre comes out clean. Cool completely on wire racks.
6. Decorate cooled cupcakes with icing and sprinkles.

*Gobble them up!*

*Never have children, only grandchildren.*
GORE VIDAL

## SUPPLIES

1 pkg white cake mix

muffin tin

tinfoil

24 flat-bottomed ice cream cones

icing (homemade or store bought)

assorted sprinkles & cake decorations

## TIP

Do not overfill the cones!

For colour, add tiny bit of food colouring gel or paste to dough and knead to combine.

Leave your creations out to harden for decorating your favourite cake.

# SIMPLE FONDANT

*Make, create and enjoy this sweet treat*

AGE • 6+        TIME • 30 MIN (+ CHILLING TIME)

1. Place marshmallows in large glass bowl.
2. Microwave on high for 40-50 seconds or until marshmallows begin to melt.
3. Stir in the water. BE CAREFUL! Gooey marshmallow will be HOT! Stir until they are completely melted.
4. Gradually add icing sugar, stirring until mixture forms sticky dough.
5. Coat your hands with butter and knead dough until smooth and no longer sticky. (Add more icing sugar if necessary.)
6. Shape dough into a ball and wrap in plastic.
7. Place in fridge for a few hours or overnight to set.
8. Sprinkle icing sugar on a flat surface and roll out dough.
9. Make shapes or cut out shapes using cookie cutters.

*Edible play dough! Yum!*

*Grandmothers are mothers with lots of frosting.* ANON

# CHILLED MINT TEA

*A cool, refreshing tea, guaranteed to make any breath minty fresh!*

AGE • 3+          TIME • 30 MIN (+ COOLING TIME)

## SUPPLIES

1 orange

1 lemon

2 1/2 c water (625 ml)

2 c sugar (500 ml)

1 c mint leaves, packed (250 ml)

ginger ale (optional)

1. Zest then slice orange and lemon. Set aside.
2. Combine water, sugar, orange and lemon slices in a saucepan. Bring to a gentle boil.
3. Simmer 5 minutes then let cool slightly.
4. Add mint and zest.
5. Squeeze juice from orange and lemon slices into saucepan.
6. Let sit for 1 hour, then strain.
7. To serve, fill teapot 1/3 full with strained syrup. Add ice if desired. Top up with water or ginger ale and pour into tea cups.

*Pinkies up!*

Dive into the Dress-Up Box, pull out your finest threads and have a tea party!

*Just about the time a woman thinks her work is done, she becomes a grandmother.*
EDWARD H. DRESCHNACK

# MARSHMALLOWS

*I made over 200 pink, heart-shaped marshmallows for our daughter's wedding. The bride and groom are still stuck on each other!* MG

AGE • 5+        TIME • 30 MIN

## SUPPLIES

1 medium-large bowl

2 tbsp gelatin (30 ml)

1/4 c cold water (60 ml)

2/3 c boiled water (150 ml)

1 1/2 c white sugar (375ml)

1/2 tsp vanilla (2 ml)

electric beater

8-inch-square baking pan (20-cm-square)

parchment paper

vegetable oil

1/2 c icing sugar (125 ml)

1 tbsp cornstarch (15 ml)

## TIPS

Use a smaller pan for thicker marshmallows.

Store in airtight container up to 1 month

1. In bowl, soak gelatin in cold water until soft (5 min).
2. Pour in boiled water and combine.
3. Stir in sugar and vanilla until sugar crystals completely dissolve.
4. With electric beater, beat on medium-high until thick and foamy, approx 10 min. Mixture will be quite sticky.
5. Line pan with parchment paper and lightly oil paper.
6. Pour mixture into pan, smooth and let set at least 1 hour.
7. With a wet knife, cut into squares
8. Mix icing sugar and cornstarch and then roll marshmallows in to coat.

*Light a bonfire, get out those sticks and let's have a marshmallow roast!*

*What a bargain grandchildren are! I give them my loose change and they give me a million dollars worth of pleasure.* GENE PERRET

Use cookie cutters to make fun shapes.

Add food colouring for festive mallows.

Roll in toasted coconut for a gourmet touch.

# FISHING GAME

*One fish, two fish, red fish, blue fish*

AGE • 3+        TIME • 30 MIN

1. Draw fish shapes on construction paper and cut out.
2. Tie yarn or string to one end of each stick.
3. Attach paper clip to free end of each length of string.
4. Tape a small magnet to each fish shape.
5. Put your fish into a bowl or lay them on floor.
6. Dangle fishing rod over those fish until your paperclip hooks a 'live one'.

*Reel them in!*

*A grandmother is a babysitter who watches the kids instead of the television...*
ANON

Number some small prizes, and number each fish. Successful fisherfolk get prize with corresponding number.

## SUPPLIES

coloured construction paper

pencil

scissors

1 chopstick or pencil per person

1-2 ft yarn or string per person

1 paperclip per fishing rod

12 small magnets

bowl (optional)

sticky tape

**!** Magnets can be a choking hazard!

# INDOOR FORT

*For hours of fun and make-believe*

AGES • 3+        TIME • 30 MIN

### SUPPLIES

sheets or light blankets

pillows

sofa cushions

comforters or sleeping bags

safety pins, clothes pegs and/or clamps

Your grandkids might like a sleepover in the fort so have flashlights and their Sweet Dreams pillows (page 28) ready.

1. Choose an area that is out of the way. You may wish to keep your fort for several days or maybe just an hour.
2. To make a basic fort, arrange chairs in a circle with backs facing in. Add more furniture for tunnels and extra rooms.
3. Drape sheets or blankets over top of chairs.
4. Use safety pins, elastics, pegs or clamps (the larger the better) to connect sheets and blankets.
5. Create a door or entrance for easy access.
6. Add a blanket and a few pillows inside to sit on. Grab a CD player or games to enjoy in your new fort.

*Great place for afternoon naps, grandparents included!*

*Grandparents don't just say "that's nice" – they reel back and roll their eyes and throw up their hands and smile. You get your money's worth out of grandparents.* ANON

# DANCING PING PONG BALLS

*The aim is to dance and wiggle the balls out of the box without using your hands!*

AGES • 3+     TIME • 15 MIN

SUPPLIES

empty tissue boxes (1 per child)

4 or more ping pong balls per box

string

timer

1. On the bottom of each tissue box, cut two small holes in corners on one long edge.
2. Pass a piece of string through holes, long enough to tie around child's waist.
3. Put 4 or more balls in each box. Opening in each box needs to be just big enough to allow balls to escape. (Use scissors to adjust size if necessary.)
4. Tie box of balls around waist of each child, resting box on lower back.
5. Set timer for 1 min to see who can 'dance and wiggle' the most balls out of box.

*Let's shake those little booties*

*On the seventh day God rested. His grandchildren must have been out of town.* GENE PERRET

With a larger number of kids, organize this as a relay race

Use coloured balls worth different points.

Have kids decorate or number their balls before game.

# Fortune Teller

*Yes, children – grandparents really do know everything!*

AGES • 5+          TIME • 30 MIN

1. Follow instructions in diagram below to make Fortune Teller.
2. Number each small triangle 1 to 8.
3. Open each flap and write a 'fortune' or funny saying in 8 small triangles.
4. Close number flaps, flip over and colour each main flap a different colour.
5. Refold along the creases several times to make Fortune Teller more pliable.
6. Fit thumbs and forefingers under coloured flaps to open and close Fortune Teller.

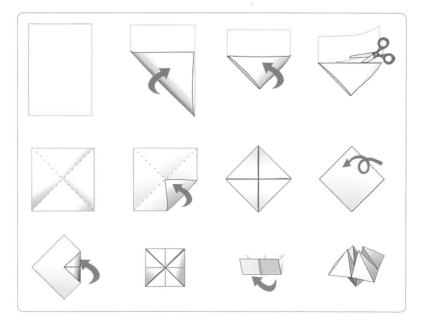

## HOW TO PLAY

1. Have your playmate choose one colour.
2. Spell out the colour as you open and close the Fortune Teller (eg B-L-U-E open and close 4 times).
3. With the Fortune Teller in an open position (fingers and thumbs spread apart), ask child to pick a number from the inside triangles.
4. Open and close the Fortune Teller that many times. End in an open position.
5. Have them pick a new number. Open the flap of that number and read out fortune they have chosen.

*Kids will love to help think up funny sayings or messages to put in the Fortune Teller.*

*One of life's greatest mysteries is how the boy who wasn't good enough to marry your daughter can be the father of the smartest grandchild in the world.* ANON

Make this classic game educational. Under the number flaps write a question and answer – math problems, animal facts, what makes up different colours, moral issues, space, etc.

# TALKING CANS

*No texting allowed! Do you remember these fun 'telephones' from your childhood? We could swear that they REALLY worked!*

AGE • 3+        TIME • 10 MIN

## SUPPLIES

2 clean, empty cans

duct tape (optional)

string

candle wax

1. Clean 2 cans and remove any sharp edges. Duct tape edges if necessary.
2. Punch a hole in bottom centre of each one.
3. Connect cans with as long a string as you decide appropriate.
4. Tie knot in string at each end to hold it in place in cans.
5. Wax string for enhanced voice connection and enjoy some free long-distance calls with your grandkids!
6. For best reception, hold string taut between cans while chatting.

*No long distance charges need apply!*

*Becoming a grandmother is wonderful. One moment you're just a mother. The next you are all-wise and prehistoric.* PAM BROWN

Let the grandkids decorate the talking cans and personalize them with pictures and letters from old magazines.

ANIMALS IN THE HOUSE, page 52

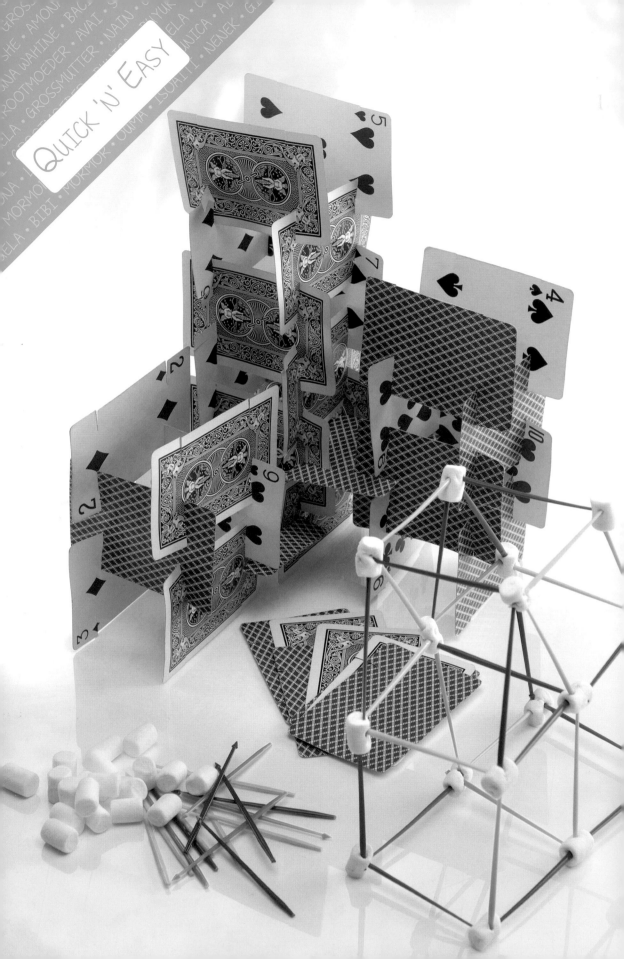

# CARD HOUSES

- Use an old pack of cards.
- On long side of each card, make 2 slits 1/2 inch deep (10 mm) into the card (3/4 inch – 15 mm – from the corner).
- Tower of cards can be created by interlocking cards at slits.

*Get ready to build your dream house!*

### TIP
To build sideways, also cut slits into shorter sides of cards.

## MARSHMALLOW ENGINEERS

- Give the grandchildren small marshmallows, a box of toothpicks and see what amazing structures they can create . . .

*. . . and then EAT!*

For added fun, use coloured marshmallows and/or coloured toothpicks.

## PRETEND CAMERA

*My two-year-old had days of fun taking pictures with her 'camera'* DB

- Kids love to take pictures! Cut out a picture of a camera, glue it to a piece of cardboard then cut out a small hole for a lens.

*Say cheese!*

# Hide a Little Toy

*Who doesn't love a surprise? Planning a visit to Noni's house always created great anticipation in our kids, who wondered what little toy she had hidden under their pillows.* DB

### TIP

Make sure toys are age appropriate. The toy can be inexpensive - the Dollar Store will become your best friend!

- Before your grandchild arrives for a sleepover, hide a little toy or treat under their pillow.
- Alternatively, hide a little love note for them to find.

*They will know you've been anticipating their visit.*

# Invisible Painting

- On a warm sunny day, collect together paint brush, rollers and/or sponges, plus a bucket for water or rolling tray.
- Give each child their own bucket and paint brush and tell them to paint driveway or outdoor furniture.
- Kids will love sloshing with the water! It will all disappear as it dries and they can start all over again.

*Now you see it, now you don't!*

# COINS IN THE GARDEN

*An excellent activity for grandparents who need a break!*

**!**

Coins are a possible choking hazard.

- Before grandkids arrive, collect a handful of coins. Count up pennies, nickels, dimes and quarters so you know totals and toss them around garden for children to find while you relax in a lawn chair.
- Kids can add up their own coins to find out if there are still more out there to search for.
- Toss coins out again if the kids enjoyed this.

*Go out somewhere to spend their treasure!*

# DANCING DIVING RAISINS

- Drop a handful of raisins (or currants) into a jar or glass of soda water.
- See if the kids can figure out what makes the raisins 'dance'. Why do some stay resting at the bottom?*

*Watch those raisins come alive!*

*Here's how you can show how smart you are: Raisins are denser than the liquid, so they sink. Carbon dioxide bubbles from the soda stick to the rough surface of a raisin, causing the raisin to rise. When the raisin reaches the surface, the bubbles pop. This causes the raisin to sink.

## MAKE YOUR OWN BUTTER

*No need to milk the cow!*

- Pour 1/2 pint (10 oz/300 ml) of whipping cream into a clear jar with a tight-fitting lid.
- Take turns shaking the jar until the butter separates from the liquid (15-30 min, depending upon how vigorously you shake). Drain off liquid.

*Use your fresh, homemade butter on bread or toast! Yummmm!*

## ANIMALS IN THE HOUSE

*Make your own set of paper animals with your grandchildren.*

- Collect magazines, calendars or old books with animal pictures that can be cut out.
- Store farm or zoo animals in self-sealing bags to be brought out for play when grandkids visit (photo page 47).

*It's fun for little ones to learn to identify animals, their sounds and names of their offspring.*

# STICKY NOTE TREASURE HUNT

*This game is great for all ages. The key is to plan out your treasure route ahead of time.*

- With yourself as start point, hand out first clue to lead them to first location.
- There, they should find second sticky note clue leading to next spot and so on, until kids reach final location.
- For non-readers, you can cut out pictures of household items (fridge, bathtub, fireplace, chair, television) from magazines or catalogues and glue them to sticky notes or draw a picture.
- You may decide to have a prize or treat at the final location or simply a note saying: "You DID it! You have reached the end!"

*Congratulations!*

*You won't be this cute forever.* ANON

Clue #1
Look in a place we keep ice cream!
Yum.....

Clue #2
Look where I rest my head at night.
zzzz

Clue #3
Look where we brush our teeth.

# WINDOW PICASSO

*Let them take their artwork home or save it as one of your treasures.*

- Remove protective backing from 1 sheet (approx 12 inch x 18 inch, 30 cm x 45 cm) clear contact paper and carefully tape sheet, sticky side out, onto window at child's shoulder height.
- Have available a variety of interesting items (bottle caps, bits of yarn, buttons, pieces of coloured tissue paper, cereal, pennies – anything lightweight enough to stick) and see what your grandkids create.
- When masterpiece is complete, peel back protective backing from another sheet of clear contact paper and place overtop, pressing firmly.

*Sure to be worth millions in the future!*

*Two things I dislike about my grand-daughter – when she won't take her afternoon nap and when she won't let me take mine.* GENE PERRET

**!**

Small items could cause a choking hazard for younger ones.

Super Soak
Detox Footbath.

Bubble Bath
Gel.

Lip
Smacking
Lip Gloss

BUBBLE BATH
GEL, page 61

SUPER SOAK
DETOX
FOOTBATH,
page 59

# LIP-SMACKING LIP GLOSS

*Pucker up for some Grandma kisses!*

AGE • 3+        TIME • 15 MIN (+ 2 HOURS TO SET)

SUPPLIES

glass bowl

1-2 tbsp petroleum jelly (15-30 ml)

1 tsp red, presweetened, flavoured drink mix (5 ml)

1-2 drops food colouring

cake glitter icing gel (optional)

small container

1. Place the petroleum jelly in a glass bowl and microwave for 20-30 sec. Remove, stir and reheat if necessary to reach a liquid state.
2. Add drink powder mix to heated jelly and combine well.
3. Add a few drops of food colouring (for a more intense colour) and a squirt of the glitter icing gel (if using). Blend well.
4. Scoop into small container. Place in fridge for 2 hours to set.

*A perfect addition to your Dress-Up Box finery. Kiss away!*

*Grandmothers never run out of hugs or cookies.* ANON

# EGG WHITE MINI-FACIAL

*Your grandchildren won't recognize their younger looking grandparent!*

AGE • 3+          TIME • 15 MIN

## SUPPLIES

small bowl

1 egg

small brush

thin white tissue paper

1. Separate egg. Save yolk for breakfast.
2. Slightly beat egg white.
3. With brush, apply egg white over face.
4. Cut a face-shaped piece of tissue paper and place over first egg-white layer on face.
5. Apply another layer of egg white.
6. Let dry completely (approx 10 min). It will feel tight.
7. Gently peel off tissue, pulling it upward.
8. Rinse and pat dry.

*Take a quick selfie before the wrinkles return!*

*There's no place like home except Grandma's.* ANON

# Super Soak Detox Footbath

*The ions in the salt act as magnets to draw toxins out of your body.*

AGE • 3+          TIME • 5 MIN

SUPPLIES

sealable plastic bag

1 c Epsom salts

1 c table salt

2 c baking soda

2-3 drops scented oil

foot basin or bucket

1. Combine ingredients in a sealable bag. Seal bag and shake to mix well.
2. Fill a bath tub, bucket or foot basin halfway with hot water.
3. Add 1/4 c of mixture to water. Stir until dissolved.
4. Submerge aching feet in lovely warm bath.

Pour ingredients into a fancy jar to make a gift.

When finished soaking, dry and paint those sparkling clean toe nails!

*Ahhhhhhhhhh......happy feet!*

*I still have my feet on the ground, I just wear better shoes.* OPRAH WINFREY

# Bubble Jelly Bath Gel

*You will be squeaky clean!*

AGE • 3+      TIME • 15 MIN (+ 4 HRS TO SOLIDIFY)

1. Sprinkle gelatin over cold water. Let sit until softened.
2. Add boiled water and stir until dissolved.
3. Pour shampoo into a separate bowl. Mix in dissolved gelatin.
4. Add food colouring, scent and Epsom salts. Mix until everything is well blended.
5. Pour into container. Refrigerate for 3-4 hours or until solidified.
6. For a bubble bath, add a few tbsp jelly to running bath water.

*Now it is time for some good clean fun!*

*They say genes skip a generation. Maybe that's why grandparents find their grandchildren so likeable.* JOAN MCINTOSH

## SUPPLIES

1 pkg unflavoured gelatin

1/4 c cold water (60 ml)

1/4 c boiled water (60 ml)

1/2 c unscented 'no-tears' shampoo (125 ml)

3-4 drops food colouring

3-4 drops scent (optional)

1-2 tsp Epsom salts, optional (5-10 ml)

decorative container or jar

Divide mixture up into a few containers and add different colours and scents to each.

This makes a great Mother's Day gift! Put it into a homemade Gift Bag, page 11.

## About the Authors

Truth be told, neither of us are grandparents yet. But, we are very enthusiastic wanna-be-grandmas and expect great things from our wonderful children before too long!

### Maureen Goulet

Crafty, crafty, that is what I have always been - forever making something. When I had my two kids, Carrie and Matthew, it gave me more opportunities for this craftiness to explode! I was making cardboard kitchens, blanket houses, tunnels, papier mâché space stations, gingerbread houses, bunny blankets and much more.

We got our crafty kids into - what else? - craft fairs where they sold candles, yo-yo balls, dog cookies and even beer bread. They were thrilled to come away with loads of real dough $$.

Two years of early childhood education, earning a Provincial Instructors diploma, and then running my own cooking school left me with no time for crafts. But now I am once again

bursting with crafty ideas and want to share them with you! I like to 'Be Prepared' so, in preparation for my grandchildren-to-be, Diana and I have poured our creative juices into this fun and useful book.

## DIANA BUDDEN

I like to regularly remind my children what a marvellous mother they have!

My own upbringing was in a busy, creative home atmosphere. Television was not an option. Playing games, creating homemade gifts, make-believe and sharing time with grandparents were the order of the day. Consequently, when my own three children were youngsters, I consciously fostered creativity in our home.

Our family had many moves as the children were growing up. I believe that our times spent together with games, crafts, baking and family outings were instrumental in keeping us close and caring as a family unit. I retain so many good memories of our shared activities.

At a later stage, I became an Orton Gillingham Tutor, working with dyslexic children at the local school.

A grandma-in-waiting, I keep busy with sports, reading and trying to find humour in everyday life. Working on this book project with Maureen has been a labour of love. We hope you enjoy the results of our efforts!

## ACKNOWLEDGEMENTS

Hats off to Kilmeny Denny and Lynn Duncan, our self-publishing gurus at Vivalogue! We would never have reached this point without their amazing help and guidance.

Huge kudos to family and friends who enthusiastically helped with assessment of all our activities and offered useful suggestions and valuable feedback.

Finally, we fully acknowledge the unwavering support of our stalwart husbands, Maurice and Neil, without whose encouragement we may have allowed this project to slide into oblivion.

# FROM THE MOUTHS OF BABES

Keep a record of great sayings from your wonderful grandchildren